MW00535249

BRAHMS

SELECTED WORKS
FOR THE PIANO

Henry Levine, **Editor**

Contents

ABOUT THIS EDITION

Alfred has made every effort to make this book not only attractive but more useful and long-lasting as well. Usually, large books do not lie flat or stay open on the piano rack. In addition, the pages (which are glued together) tend to break away from the spine after repeated use.

In this edition, pages are sewn together in multiples of 16. This special process allows the book to stay open for ease in playing and prevents pages from falling out. We hope this unique binding will give you added pleasure and additional use.

Second Edition

Copyright © MCMXCII by Alfred Music

All rights reserved.

THEMATIC INDEX

Johannes BRAHMS

born in Hamburg, May 7, 1833
settled in Vienna in 1862
died in Vienna, April 3, 1897

BRAHMS — as Composer

In the history of music it is not unusual to find composers who did not at first receive favorable recognition. Nicolas Slonimsky, who has recorded critical assaults on many now famous composers in his *Lexicon of Musical Invective,* characterized such criticisms as "Non-Acceptance of the Unfamiliar." Brahms received his share of critical blasts. One of these, a biting criticism from Tchaikovsky, entered in his Diary of October 9, 1886, reads:

> "I played over the music of that scoundrel Brahms. What a giftless . . . . . .! It annoys me that this self-inflated mediocrity is hailed as a genius. Why in comparison with him, Raff is a giant, not to speak of [Anton] Rubinstein, who is after all a live and important human being, while Brahms is chaotic and absolutely dried-up stuff."

Brahms fared better with Liszt. As a young man of twenty, Brahms was introduced to Liszt, who played over the early piano pieces that Brahms had brought along. Liszt was favorably impressed with him as a composer, but did not have a high regard for him as a pianist. On the other hand, Brahms, who had a high regard for Liszt, the pianist, as a super-technician, did not share the general enthusiasm for Liszt as a composer. The story is told that when Liszt played his own Sonata for Brahms and an admiring group, Brahms dozed off. (William Mason, an American pupil of Liszt, was present on this occasion and writes about it in his *Memoirs of a Musical Life.*)

Musical Vienna, in the late 1860's, was divided into two antagonistic musical groups—the pro-Brahms and the pro-Wagner. The followers in each group sang the praises of their own idol and disparaged the idol of the other group. Among the admirers of Brahms were the famous Vienna music critic, Eduard Hanslick, the great violinist, Joseph Joachim, who had sent Brahms to Liszt, and Robert and Clara Schumann. Robert Schumann, in his musical journal, the *Neue Zeitschrift für Musik,* heralded the genius of the young Brahms. Clara Schumann, for whom Brahms felt an almost filial affection, championed his piano works and featured them in her public recitals.

Today, of course, Brahms is recognized as one of the musical giants—one of the great three B's of music, as von Bülow put it—Bach, Beethoven, Brahms. The piano music of Brahms has its own distinctive pianistic texture, rich in melodic and harmonic invention, in rhythmic resourcefulness, in tonal color and poetic and dramatic mood. But his music requires a special form of piano technique.

BRAHMS—his Piano Writing

Brahms suffered not only from critics as a composer but from pianists who judged his piano writing awkward and unplayable. The great piano pedagogue, Theodor Leschetizky (1830-1915), a contemporary of Brahms, had misgivings about Brahms' style of writing for the piano. Edwine Behre, one of his American pupils, relates that when she brought to a lesson the Brahms Intermezzo in e-flat minor, Op. 118, No. 6, of which she was very fond, Leschetizky exclaimed, "Warum spielen Sie das unklaviermässige Zeug?" ("Why do you play that unpianistic stuff?")

Ethel Newcomb, in her book, *Leschetizky As I Knew Him*, quotes him as saying, "Brahms always troubles me. He had no regard for the piano as an instrument." She writes further that when they were together Brahms made fun of Leschetizky's compositions and Leschetizky made fun of Brahms' piano pieces. Nevertheless, Leschetizky eventually became a great admirer of Brahms and taught many of his piano works.

To the complaints about his piano writing style, Brahms answered (italics mine):

> "I have no patience with the pianist who growls because of a few *new technical difficulties*. Shall progress stop because of a few *hard nuts* to crack?

All my life I have been deeply interested in piano technique, and I have endeavored in my piano works to combine good musical ideas with *new idioms*. You will find the *new technique* more particularly in my Paganini Variations and in my Capriccio. I admit that many of the passages lie awkwardly for the hands. This *new kind of technique* seems inconvenient ('unbequem' was the word he used) because hands and fingers are used in a *new way*. The *new idiom* requires greater strength, freedom and independence of fingers than the traditional classical piano technique."

Of course, it would have helped if Brahms had explained his "new" piano technique. Since he had not, we are left to our own conjectures based on a technical study of his piano compositions and an understanding of muscular properties. For, in the last analysis, Brahms was doing something that was physically possible, at least to him, though it may have been a secret to other pianists.

Brahms had evolved a style of writing for the piano that required, as he had declared, great freedom and bold abandon. For example,

from the Rhapsody in E flat, Op. 119, No. 4

leaps in the right hand:

from the Rhapsody in g minor, Op. 79, No. 2

leaps in the left hand (at x)

At the x's, the leaps may be made, close to the keys, by applying a principle of kinesiology, the science of bodily movement. This principle states that when a sidewise movement to the left or right is no more than an octave the movement may be made only by the forearm, from a stationary elbow, without a sidewise displacement of the upper arm from the shoulder. Test this: Hold a book between the upper arm and body (to prevent movement of the upper arm sidewise), and "flip" the forearm sidewise to the left or right. Try this device on the passages on page 4, first with the held book then without it. (This trick is used by rag-time players in playing a "swing" bass.) In wider leaps the upper arm may come into play.

The Brahms piano writing style has also been criticized for its thickness of tonal texture. On paper the music does look full of notes. And it can sound thick and muddy, unless the player aims for a proper tonal voicing and perspective whereby the melody is kept in the foreground, the flowing and involved accompaniment in the background, and a dynamic balance maintained between the hands. Then the music will sound rich and clear, with a distinctive Brahmsian tonal glow.

> Editorial suggestions have been added as to pedaling and fingering. In a very few places Brahms has indicated his own fingering, shown in italics in this volume. I have added fingerings for passages that seem complicated. Despite criticisms of his awkward writing style, the notes that Brahms wrote do lie under the fingers.

HEMIOLA

A favorite rhythmic pattern with Brahms was the *hemiola*. The word is derived from the Greek *hemiolios*, meaning half as much again (hemi + holos = half + whole = 1½ = $\frac{3}{2}$; in music, 3 against 2).

The hemiola is based on the fact that 6 eighths may be divided into 2 groups of 3 eighths, as in $\frac{6}{8}$ ♩♩♩ ♩♩♩ or ♩. ♩. or into 3 groups of 2 eighths, as in $\frac{3}{4}$ ♩♩ ♩♩ ♩♩ or ♩ ♩ ♩ The eighth note is the common time-unit.

The hemiola may be used 1) simultaneously or 2) consecutively. Brahms used it both ways.

1) hemiola, used simultaneously (between the hands, or in each hand):

> page 24, bottom brace, first 3 measures (hemiola between hands)
>
> page 25, top brace, last measure (hemiola between hands)
>
> page 26, 3rd brace, 1st measure (hemiola in l.h.)
>
> page 26, 3rd brace, 2nd measure (hemiola in each hand)
>
> page 27, 3rd brace, last measure (hemiola in r.h. and between hands)
>
> page 51, 1st brace, last measure (hemiola between hands)
>
> page 51, 2nd brace, 1st measure (hemiola between hands)

2) hemiola, used consecutively ($\frac{6}{8}$ followed by $\frac{3}{4}$, felt but not indicated):

> page 52, 1st brace, 2nd measure
>
> page 52, 3rd brace, 3rd measure
>
> page 80, 2nd brace, 4th measure
>
> page 82, last brace, 1st measure

Henry Levine

For a comprehensive account of the life and works of Brahms, see *The Life of Johannes Brahms*, in two volumes, by Florence May. (William Reeves, London.)

BALLADE
("EDWARD")*
D MINOR

Johannes Brahms, Op. 10, No. 1

*After the Scottish ballad "Edward", in Herder's "Stimmen der Völker" ("Folk Songs").

Tempo I

BALLADE
G MINOR

Allegro energico

Op. 118, No. 3

*Brahms fingering in italics

CAPRICCIO
B MINOR

Op. 76, No. 2

Allegretto non troppo

poco - a - poco - più tranquillo
espress. r. h.

sempre dolce

later editions

INTERMEZZO
Eb MAJOR

Op. 117, No. 1

1) Schlaf sanft, mein Kind, schlaf sanft und schön!
Mich dauert's sehr, dich weinen sehn.
(Schottisch, Aus Herder's Volksliedern)

Andante moderato

1) Sleep soft, my bairn, now sweetly sleep,
My heart is wae to see thee weep.
(Scottish, from Herder's Folk Songs)

*Hemiola. See page 5.

Più adagio

pp sempre ma molto espressivo

*Hemiola. See page 5.

Un poco più andante

*Hemiola. See page 5.

1) Lower voice, beginning on 3rd beat, imitates upper voice which began on 1st beat.

*Hemiola. See page 5.

INTERMEZZO
Bb MINOR

Op. 117, No. 2

Andante non troppo e con molta espressione

INTERMEZZO
A MINOR

Op. 118, No. 1
(1893)

Allegro non assai, ma molto appassionato

INTERMEZZO
A MAJOR

Op. 118, No. 2

Andante teneramente

INTERMEZZO
Eb MINOR

Op. 118, No. 6

Andante, largo e mesto

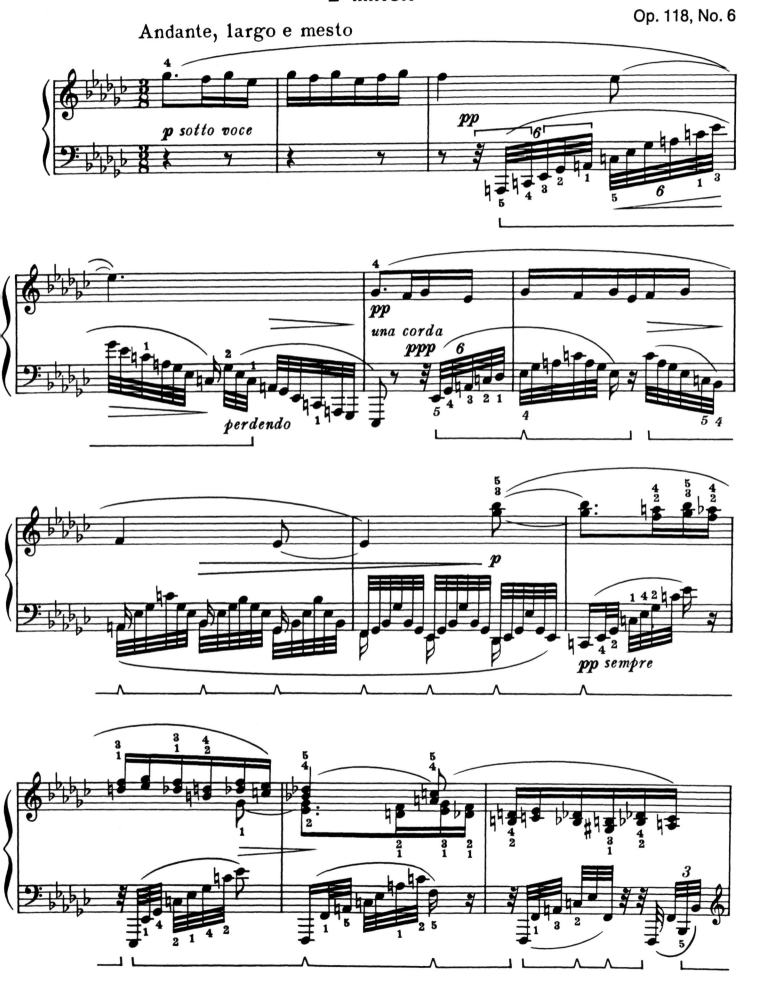

INTERMEZZO
C MAJOR

Op. 119, No. 3

*Hemiola. See page 5.

*Hemiola. See page 5.

RHAPSODY
B MINOR

Op. 79, No. 1
(1880)

poco   *a*   *poco*   *ri -*

dim. poco a poco

r. h.

- - tar - - dan - - do - - - - - - -

r. h.

pp

RHAPSODY
G MINOR

Op. 79, No. 2

Molto passionato, ma non troppo allegro

1) Let the ♩ be the time unit. By dividing it into 6 eighths, then into 4 eighths, then into 3 quarters, then into 2 quarters, the effect of a ritardando (quasi. rit.) is obtained, without changing the tempo.

RHAPSODY
E♭ MAJOR

Op. 119, No. 4

Allegro risoluto

*Hemiola. See page 5.

1) Fingering in italics by Brahms.

*Hemiola. See page 5.

1) Fingering in italics by Brahms.

WALTZ

Ab MAJOR

Op. 39, No. 15

Grazioso

p dolce

poco cresc.

GAVOTTE IN A
BY C. W. VON GLUCK

Transcribed by Brahms

*Notes with up-stem played with R.H.

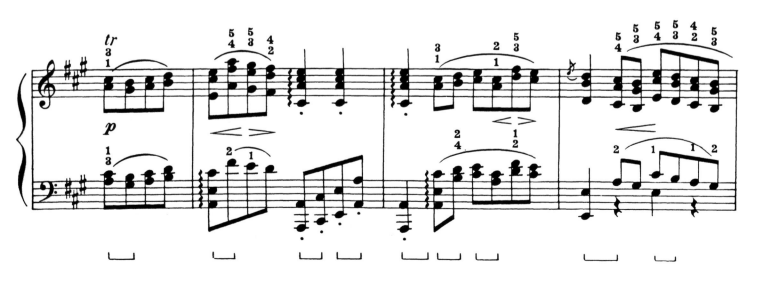

HUNGARIAN DANCE
NO. 7, IN F MAJOR

Allegretto vivace